Gratitude

About The Cover

Native Americans believe that Hummingbirds were created from flowers, and return each spring to express their eternal gratitude to flowers of all kinds...

This Book Belongs To:

Gratitude...Noun
The Quality Of Being Thankful; Readiness
To Show Appreciation For,
And To Return Kindness...

Gratitude Unlocks The Fullness Of Life...

This Day I Am Grateful For:

_____

_____

_____

It's A Good Day
To Be Grateful...

This Day I Am Grateful For:

_____

_____

_____

Begin Each Day With A Grateful Heart...

This Day I Am Grateful For:

_____

_____

_____

A Grateful Heart
Attracts Miracles…

This Day I Am Grateful For:

_____

_____

_____

Start Each Day With A Grateful Smile...

This Day I Am Grateful For:

_____

_____

_____

Be Obsessively Grateful...

This Day I Am Grateful For:

_____

_____

_____

The Simplest Form
Of Gratitude is Joy...

This Day I Am Grateful For:

_____

_____

_____

The Essence Of All Beautiful Art, All Great Art, Is Gratitude...

This Day I Am Grateful For:

_____

_____

_____

Gratitude Is Riches...

This Day I Am Grateful For:

_____

_____

_____

Always Have An Attitude Of Gratitude...

This Day I Am Grateful For:

_____

_____

_____

Gratitude Changes Everything...

This Day I Am Grateful For:

_____

_____

_____

If You Want Happiness,
Find Gratitude...

This Day I Am Grateful For:

_____

_____

_____

Gratitude Turns What We Have Into Enough...

This Day I Am Grateful For:

_____

_____

_____

Enough Is A Feast...

This Day I Am Grateful For:

_____

_____

_____

Thankfulness Is The Beginning Of Gratitude.
Gratitude Is The Completion Of Thankfulness...

This Day I Am Grateful For:

_____

_____

_____

Let Us Be Grateful To The People Who Make Us Happy...

This Day I Am Grateful For:

_____

_____

_____

Be Mindful And Grateful...

This Day I Am Grateful For:

_____

_____

_____

Gratitude Is Abundance...

This Day I Am Grateful For:

_____

_____

_____

Be Grateful For Every Good Thing That Comes To You...

This Day I Am Grateful For:

_____

_____

_____

There Is A Calmness To A Life Lived In Gratitude...

This Day I Am Grateful For:

_____

_____

_____

Gratitude Is A Choice...

This Day I Am Grateful For:

_____

_____

_____

Dream Big, Be Grateful...

This Day I Am Grateful For:

_____

_____

_____

Focus On Gratitude
And A Path Will Open
For You...

This Day I Am Grateful For:

_____

_____

_____

*Gratitude Is The Sign Of
Noble Souls...*

This Day I Am Grateful For:

In Everything, Give

Thanks...

This Day I Am Grateful For:

_____

_____

_____

Learn To Be Thankful For What You Already Have...

This Day I Am Grateful For:

_____

_____

_____

Through The Eyes Of Gratitude, Everything Is A Miracle...

This Day I Am Grateful For:

_____

_____

_____

Gratitude Brings Joy And Laughter Into Your Life...

This Day I Am Grateful For:

Gratitude Is The Ability To Experience Life As A Gift...

This Day I Am Grateful For:

_____

_____

_____

Your Struggle Ends When Gratitude Begins...

This Day I Am Grateful For:

_____

_____

_____

Be Grateful...

CJF

Made in the USA
Las Vegas, NV
22 October 2023